The Abandoned ...
by Simon ...

THE CAST

Sam

Mouse

Jojo

Ben

Josh
Ben's father

Tessa
Ben's sister

Policewoman

Sergeant Thomas
Policeman

TV voice

Scene 1

On the common. Sam, Jojo, Mouse and Ben are on their bikes.

Sam   Let's leave the bikes here and go into the woods.

Mouse   Do you reckon it'll be all right to go in? We might get into trouble.

Sam   Don't be such a baby, Mouse. Come on, let's explore.

Sam goes into the woods.

Ben   I've been in these woods before and there's a great stream for messing about in. I say we go in. You coming, Jojo?

Jojo   Might as well.

Sam calls from inside the wood.

Sam   *(Off)* Oh, wow! Come and see what I've found!

Ben   Where are you, Sam?

Sam   Over here. Down in the dip. Hurry up – you're not going to believe this.

Ben runs off.

Jojo   Come on, Mouse.

Mouse   I'm coming.

Jojo runs off, followed by Mouse.

Scene 2

Seconds later. Inside the woods. Sam, Ben, Mouse and Jojo are gathered around an abandoned car. They look in through the windows.

Ben It must have been stolen and dumped here.

Mouse Look. They've smashed a window. That's probably how they got in.

Jojo How could they drive it without the keys?

Sam It must be easy enough if you know how. I expect it only takes a car thief a minute.

Jojo But it's all scratched and bashed. And it's a really nice car.

Ben GTI Turbo, fuel injection, 24-valve, six-speed gearbox. I want one just like this when I'm older, only in silver.

Sam opens the driver's door.

Ben Careful, Sam. We ought to leave it alone.
Sam gets in.

Sam Why? It's abandoned. Anyone fancy a spin?
Sam pretends to be driving and makes engine noises.

Sam Brrrrrrrm. Nyeeeeeaoow.
Ben climbs into the passenger seat. Mouse and Jojo get into the back.

Mouse Mind that broken glass, Jojo.

Ben *(Excitedly)* We mustn't tell anyone else about this. This can be our second secret place.

Jojo It'll make a great den.

Mouse The police will probably be looking for it, if it's stolen.

Scene 2

Jojo It might not be from round here. Anyway, it'll be ages before anyone else comes through these woods. That's why they dumped it here. What do you reckon, Sam?
Sam is still pretending to be driving. She pulls on the steering wheel as if she is throwing the car round bends, making tyre screeching noises. Gradually all the others join in her game.

Sam *(Like an angry parent)* Don't put me off when I'm driving!

Ben *(Shouts)* Keep your eyes on the road!

Sam *(Shouts back)* I don't need your advice – you just read the map. Which way do I turn here?

Ben Right! No, left! Take a left here!
Sam makes more screeching noises and pulls hard on the wheel.

Ben You idiot! You could have killed us there!

Sam Look at this old chap ahead of us.

Mouse Beep the horn at him.

Sam Beep! Beep! Get out of our way!

All Roadhog!

Ben *(Turning round to Mouse and Jojo)* Be quiet in the back, you pesky kids.

Scene 2

Mouse and Jojo now play-act at being the children in the back of the family car.

Mouse *(Whining)* Are we nearly there yet?

Ben No!

Jojo *(Whining)* When will be halfway?

Ben Later.

Mouse I'm bored.

Jojo We're bored.

Sam *(Pretending to be really angry)* If I hear any more from you two, I'll stop the car, put you out and leave you by the side of the road. Is that clear?

Mouse *(Pointing at Jojo)* But she keeps hitting me.

Jojo He started it.

Scene 2

Sam I warned you. I'll stop and put you out. I really mean it.

Ben She means it.

Jojo *(Whining)* I need to go to the toilet.

Sam Right. That's it. I'm stopping right here. I've had just about enough of you horrible kids.
They stop the game and laugh.

Jojo This is a good laugh. Can I have a go in the front seat now, Sam?
Ben opens the glove compartment and finds a bag.

Ben What's in here? *(He looks in the bag and pulls out a handful of jewellery.)* Wow – look at all this stuff! Necklaces and rings and earrings and all sorts. There's tons of jewellery in here. It must be worth loads.

Scene 2

Mouse Let's see. Cor, look! This is made of gold.

Jojo And these are diamond earrings. *(Tries them on)* How do I look?

Ben Take them off, Jojo. They're probably stolen goods. I expect some burglars used this as a getaway car and dumped it here.

Sam You know what that means, don't you?

Mouse
Jojo } What?
Ben

Scene 2

Sam They'll be coming back for the jewellery later.

Jojo We don't know that. Maybe the stuff was here before the car was stolen. Maybe someone's lost their car *and* their jewellery.

Mouse There could be a massive reward.

Sam We should hide the jewellery somewhere safe. Then, if there's a reward, we get it.

Mouse Hmmm. Not sure about that.

Sam It's not like we're stealing it, more like we're keeping it safe. And it's much better than letting the burglars come back for it. Anyway, I'm not missing out on any reward. Look – it fits into my rucksack easily.
(She stuffs the jewellery into her rucksack.)

Scene 2

Mouse What'll you do with it, Sam?

Sam Hide it here, inside this old tree. *(Puts the rucksack in the hollow of a tree)* But we must all swear not to tell anyone.

Mouse
Jojo } Swear.
Ben

Sam Until we *all* agree to tell.

Mouse
Jojo } Until we all agree. Swear.
Ben

Scene 2

Scene 3

The evening of the same day. The front room in Ben's house. Ben is sitting on the sofa, reading. His father, Josh, is tidying up.

Enter Tessa.

Tessa Ben, switch on the telly. Let's see what's on.

Josh Leave him, Tessa. Can't you see he's reading quietly?

Tessa *(Sulkily)* Well, he should go to his room if he wants to read, shouldn't he, because I want to watch the telly now.

Josh Have you done all your homework?

Tessa Of course I have. *(To Ben)* Come on, switch it on.
Ben uses the remote control to switch on the television. Josh goes out of the room.

TV voice Police in Wellbridge are investigating a robbery from a jewellers in the town centre …

Tessa The news. Boring. Change the channel.

Ben Shhh. Wait a minute.

TV voice … say that thieves broke into the High Street shop at around two o'clock this morning, taking with them ten thousand pounds' worth of jewellery. Police are appealing for witnesses …

Tessa Give me the remote. I don't want to watch the news.

Ben No, wait. Shhh …

TV voice … offering a generous reward for information leading to the recovery of the stolen goods. Members of the public are asked to contact local police on this number: 08 …

Tessa grabs the remote control and switches over to another channel.

Scene 3

Ben *(Sarcastically)* Oh thanks a lot, Tessa. I was interested in that story.

Tessa Oh yeah? I suppose you think you're going to solve that crime for the police, are you?

Ben Might do.

Tessa Huh! Ace detective Sherlock King saves the day! I don't think so!

Ben *(Angrily)* You think you're so smart but you don't know anything.

Ben storms out of the room.

Scene 3

Scene 4

The next morning. Inside the secret room in Castle Park. Ben, Mouse, Jojo and Sam are sitting in a huddle, talking quietly.

Ben So did anyone else see the news about the jewellery robbery?

Sam I saw it.

Mouse We didn't, but Mum and Dad were talking about it over tea.

Jojo So what are we going to do?

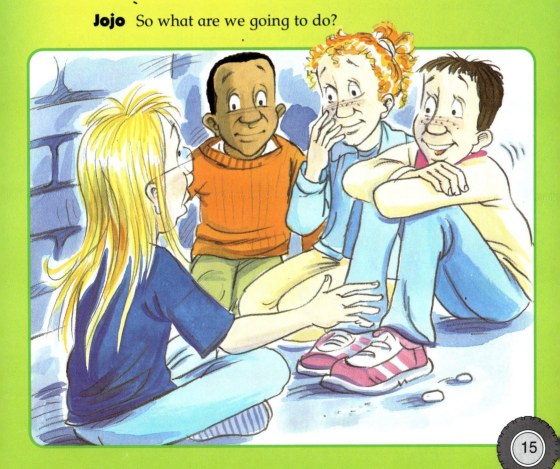

Ben I suppose we ought to tell the police and hand the stuff in. That way we can help them to catch the crooks.

Sam But then they'll find out about the car and we won't be able to play in it any more. And it's going to make such a good den.

Jojo Can't we just keep it a secret for a few more days and then tell the police?

Mouse We could get in trouble if we don't tell anyone.

Ben It does seem a shame that we could never play in the car again. It was such good fun.

Jojo Perhaps we could keep quiet about it for a day or two. What do you think?

Sam Let's just go down to the woods and have another look at it. The police might've found it anyway. And if they haven't, well it's all ours for a few more days.

Ben So who wants to go back down to the car?

Sam What're we waiting for?

Scene 4

Scene 4

Scene 5

Later that day. In the woods by the abandoned car.

Enter Sam, Mouse, Jojo and Ben.

Sam See. I told you the police wouldn't have found it yet.

Mouse How do you know they haven't?

Sam Because if they had, they'd have stuck one of those big stickers on it, you know the ones – 'Police Aware'. Besides, they would probably tow it away.
Jojo goes into the car. She is playing around in the driver's seat.

Jojo It's really comfy in here. Pity we can't get the radio to work.
Sam, Ben and Mouse join her in the car.

Ben Yeah, if we had the keys, we could play tapes and use the heater and stuff like that.

Sam That doesn't matter. If we want it as a den, we could bring our own things down here. Food and drink and stuff. And I could bring down my tape player.

Mouse What's this on the floor?

Ben What?
Mouse picks up a glove.

Mouse Look. A glove.

Sam What about it?

Mouse Well, was it here yesterday? Did anyone notice it then?

Sam I can't remember.

Mouse But think. Did anyone see it?
Long silence.

Ben Maybe the burglars came back to the car last night to look for the jewels. Perhaps one of them left the glove behind.

Jojo Why would they bring a glove to look in the car?

Scene 5

Ben Because they don't want to leave their fingerprints all over the car.

Jojo quickly takes her hands off the wheel and wipes it hard with her jumper.

Jojo Oh no. Our prints will be all over the place. We'll have to try and wipe them off.

Mouse, Sam and Ben start wiping furiously with their sleeves.

Sam *(Cheerfully)* That should do the job.

Ben You must be joking. They've got all sorts of equipment to find fingerprints. They're bound to find hundreds. If we're not careful, they'll think it was us who stole the car.

Mouse We'd better go to the police.

Ben They'll believe us if we tell them the whole story.

Mouse And besides, we wouldn't want to meet the burglars if they came back for their loot.

Jojo That's true!

Mouse And think of the reward.

Sam Hmmm. I suppose so. A bit of extra cash would come in handy.

Jojo How do we give the jewels over to the police?

Scene 5

Ben I suppose we just walk into the police station and tell them everything.

Mouse Won't we get in to trouble for playing in the stolen car?

Ben Maybe. But at least we'll be doing the right thing. The robbers might strike again, if they aren't caught soon.

Sam All right. Let's get down to the police station.

Ben Are we all agreed?

Mouse
Jojo } Agreed.
Sam

Scene 5

Scene 6

An hour later. The police station. A Policewoman (WPC) stands behind the counter, filling in a form.

Enter Sam, Mouse, Jojo and Ben. They look nervous. Sam is clutching her rucksack.

WPC Good morning, boys and girls. What can I do for you?

Ben Well ... we've solved a crime.

WPC *(Puts down her pen and looks very interested)* Ah-ha. Perhaps you'd like to tell me some more about it.
Long silence.

WPC Come on then, don't be shy.
Ben, Mouse, Jojo and Sam all speak at the same time, very quickly.

Ben Down in the woods ...

Mouse All the missing jewels ...

Jojo The High Street robbery ...

Sam The news on the telly ...

Sam And we've come to claim the reward.

WPC *(Smiling)* I'm sorry if I'm being a bit slow to catch on here, but I'm not quite sure I'm following this story. Can I have one of you at a time?

Scene 6

Sam We've got something here that you might be interested in. *(She puts the rucksack down on the counter.)*

WPC A rucksack?

Sam takes out the bag and tips all the jewellery out onto the counter.

Sam I expect you've been looking all over the area for this, haven't you?

WPC picks up the items and examines them slowly.

WPC Hmmm.

Scene 6

Ben And we hear there's a big reward on offer.

WPC *(Smiling)* I wouldn't count on it if I were you.

Sam But we saw it on the telly. The report on the news about the big robbery in the High Street.

WPC Ah, now I see.

Jojo And we've found the jewels.

WPC Oh, right, I'm with you. Look, you chaps just wait here a second while I have a word with my boss. *WPC goes out. Mouse, Jojo, Ben and Sam talk quietly among themselves.*

Sam How much do you reckon the reward will be?

Jojo I don't know. Probably about a hundred pounds.

Scene 6

Mouse So we'd get thirty pounds each!

Sam Twenty-five pounds, actually. Still, think what we could buy with that.

Jojo D'you think they'll pay us in cash or will they write cheques out to our parents?
Loud laughter from the office. The WPC returns to the counter.

Sam Are we going to get our reward now?

WPC Oh, sure. Are you going to be all right carrying it home in that rucksack of yours?

Sam Yeah!

WPC Well, let me see. One reward coming right up.
WPC looks under the counter. Comes up with four chocolate bars which she hands over to the children. Sam, Mouse, Jojo and Ben look very disappointed.

Ben Is that it? But on the telly they said something about a big reward.

WPC Yes, but that reward is for the jewels from the High Street break-in last night.

Jojo You mean, this isn't the same stuff?

WPC No, I'm afraid not. What you found is called costume jewellery. The cheap and cheerful kind, if you get my drift. Nothing wrong with it, mind, it's still very nice.

Scene 6

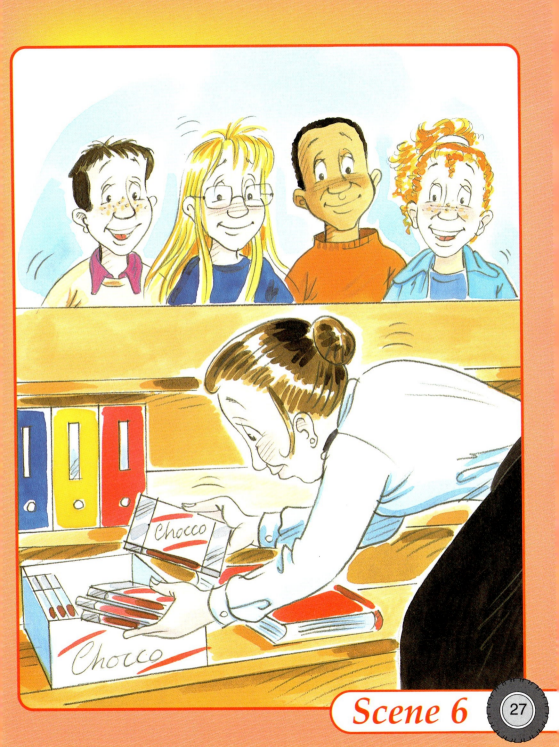

Jojo And it's not worth thousands of pounds?

WPC *(Laughs)* Oh no! I expect you could pick this lot up for ten pounds in the market.

Mouse Ten pounds! Huh! We thought it must be gold because it was hidden in the getaway car.

WPC Getaway car? What's that, then?
Long silence from the children.

WPC Come on, lad ... what's all this about a getaway car?

Mouse *(Shyly)* Well, we found this car ... it was kind of hidden in the woods. At first we just thought it would make a good den.

WPC Yes?

Mouse One of the back windows was broken, like it had been stolen.

WPC Any idea what kind of car it was?

Sam Well, it was red ...

Ben ... GTI Turbo, fuel injection, 24-valve, six-speed gearbox.

WPC Very interesting. And where did you say you found it?

Sam In the woods on the common.

WPC I'll tell you what. You chaps might just have earned yourselves a little reward yet.

Scene 6

Jojo Why? Are you looking for that car?

WPC We certainly are. *(Calls over her shoulder into the main office.)* Sergeant Thomas – can you spare us a minute out here?

Enter Sergeant Thomas.

WPC We've got some visitors with a bit of good news for you.

Scene 6

Sergeant (SGT) Oh yes. Morning, kids. I know you, don't I? You're from Story Street School and I visited your class last term. How are you all doing?

Children *(Mumbling)* All right, Sergeant Thomas.

SGT So what's this good news you're bringing me? You thinking of joining the police force?

WPC It looks like they've found our missing vehicle for us, Sarge.

SGT *(Very pleased)* Have they now? Well, that is good news indeed. You've done us a very big favour there, if you've got the right car.

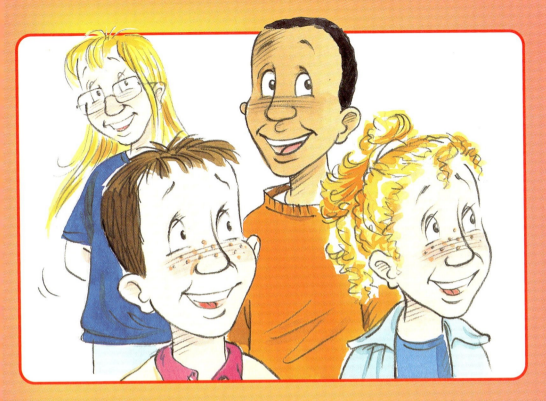

WPC No doubt about that, if our young car expert here is right.

SGT Perhaps you'd like to take us out to see the car?

Jojo It's quite a way.

Ben I expect we'd need to go by car.

SGT *(Laughs)* I know what you're getting at. You want a lift in the squad car, don't you?

Ben Well, if we can …

WPC Come on, then. Follow me. I'll drive you all out there.

Scene 6

Sam Yessss!

Ben Can I sit in the front seat?

Jojo Can we put the siren on?

Mouse And the flashing lights?

WPC We'll have to see about that.

Ben *(Pleading)* Oh, go on. Just for a bit.

WPC Well, maybe. If you behave yourselves. Are you coming then?

Children Yes!

Exit WPC followed by all the children.

Scene 6